INSIDE!

YOUR AWESOME MATCH ANNUAL 2013!

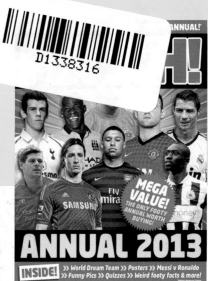

ANNUAL 2013

INSIDE! ›› World Dream Team ›› Posters ›› Messi v Ronaldo
›› Funny Pics ›› Quizzes ›› Weird footy facts & more!

MEGA VALUE! THE ONLY FOOTY ANNUAL WORTH BUYING!

WORLD DREAM TEAM 24

EURO 2012 REVIEW 58

TOP TEN 44

MESSI v RONALDO 46

PREMIER LEAGUE SCRAPBOOK 68

STRANGE BUT TRUE 78

SUBSCRIBE TO MATCH – TURN TO PAGE 95 FOR MORE INFO!

HERE COMES 2013!

MATCH checks out the wicked footy coming your way next year!

TITLE RACE!

Both Manchester giants will be battling it out for the 2012-13 Prem title, but watch out for big-spending Chelsea, Arsenal's new signings, Tottenham's stars and Liverpool's new-look team too!

TOP STRIKERS!

The Prem is packed with explosive goal machines who want to bag the Golden Boot! Rooney's desperate to win it after never finishing as top scorer, but Van Persie, Cisse, Aguero, Suarez and Torres all love ripping the net too!

CUP FINALS!

Feb. 24	Capital One Cup
Apr. 7	Johnstone's Paint Trophy
May 11	FA Cup
May 15	Europa League
May 18	League 2 Play-Off
May 19	League 1 Play-Off
May 25	Champions League
May 27	Championship Play-Off

What are you most looking forward to in 2013? Have your say on MATCH's Facebook page now!

CHAMPIONS LEAGUE!

Just two years after Barça beat Man. United in London, the biggest final in Europe is back at Wembley! It'll be a record seventh time the home of footy has hosted the match! Can an English team win it again?

WORLD CUP QUALIFIERS!

The road to Brazil 2014 is well underway and the home nations want to be there! Scotland face Wales and Northern Ireland battle Russia in March, Republic Of Ireland go to Germany in October and England travel to Ukraine in September!

CRUNCH CLASHES!

Jan. 12	Arsenal v Man. City
Jan. 12	Man. United v Liverpool
Jan. 19	Chelsea v Arsenal
Jan. 19	Tottenham v Man. United
Feb. 2	Man. City v Liverpool
Feb. 23	Man. City v Chelsea
Mar. 2	Tottenham v Arsenal
Apr. 6	Man. United v Man. City
Apr. 13	Newcastle v Sunderland
Apr. 27	Arsenal v Man. United
May 4	Liverpool v Everton
May 4	Man. United v Chelsea

RU 2 BROTHERS?

MATCH LOOKS AT SOME OF THE BEST LOOKALIKES OF THE YEAR!

GIANFRANCO ZOLA
WATFORD BOSS

"I'M MUCH BETTER LOOKING!"

BEN STILLER
ACTOR

"SHUT IT, BEN!"

DAVID DUNN
BLACKBURN

STEVE BACKSHALL
DEADLY 60 PRESENTER

"I'D BE GREAT ON TV!"

ZLATAN IBRAHIMOVIC
PSG

IAN THORPE
OLYMPICS PUNDIT

"NO WAY, MY HAIR'S BETTER!"

LUIS SUAREZ
LIVERPOOL

"WHAT ARE YOU TRYING TO SAY?"

DONKEY
SHREK

CELEBRITY FANS!
MO FARAH

Olympic 5,000 and 10,000m gold medalist Mo Farah is a massive Arsenal fan!

"I'D TRADE THIS FOR A PREM TITLE!"

BIRTHDAY CORNER!

MLADEN PETRIC

Is 32 on New Year's Day!

WEIRD BEARD!

"IT LOOKS GREAT, MATCH!"

Juventus playmaker Andrea Pirlo looked hairier than Chewbacca after sprouting a mega beard after Euro 2012!

DAVID DE GEA
MAN. UNITED

ALPACA
HAIRY ANIMAL

MY HAIR'S NOT LIKE THAT!

HEY, THE JOKE'S ON HIM!

SAMIR NASRI
MAN. CITY

MICHAEL McINTYRE
COMEDIAN

THAT TRACKSUIT SUCKS!

VICENTE DEL BOSQUE
SPAIN BOSS

MR. POTATO HEAD
TOY STORY

FANS!

Get a load of these footy fans from London 2012!

BRAZIL

JAPAN

TEAM GB

URUGUAY

NEW ZEALAND

STARS' CARS!

Jermaine Pennant
Chrome Aston Martin DBS

Costs: £130,000
0-60: 4.3 seconds
Top Speed: 191mph

WAG WATCH!

Check out Ronaldo's smoking-hot babe Irina Shayk!

Raheem Sterling...
THE NEXT BIG THING!

MATCH chats to 17-year-old *LIVERPOOL* wonderkid *RAHEEM STERLING*, who's set to become a megastar in 2013!

STERLING STATS!

CROSSING		8
PACE		9
DRIBBLING		9
SHOOTING		8
TRICKS		8
STRENGTH		6

FLYING WINGER!

RAHEEM SAYS: "I started off playing as an attacking right or left wing-back, but I'm definitely a left winger now. Ideally, I like playing on the left of the three in a 4-2-3-1 formation where I sit off the shoulder of the striker."

SPECIAL SKILLS!

RAHEEM SAYS: "My strengths are my pace and dribbling. I like to express myself on the ball and obviously create chances for the team. I've also got pretty good technique and I've got a few tricks up my sleeve, which I use to unbalance my opponents."

PLAYING STYLE!

RAHEEM SAYS: "People like to compare me to Aaron Lennon in the way I play, and I think I am quite like him. Although when I did athletics at school I could run the 100 metres in 10.99 seconds, so I'd like to think I'm probably a bit nippier than he is!"

LOADS OF GOALS!

RAHEEM SAYS: "I started out at a team called Alpha Omega in the Hillingdon area of London when I was 10 years old, before QPR offered me a trial. When I was 13, I remember hitting 50 goals in a season for my age group and the next year I was moved up to play in the Under-18s!"

LIVERPOOL MOVE!

RAHEEM SAYS: "I remember rumours going around that other clubs were interested in me when I was at school, but when Liverpool put in a bid I just signed for them. It's a massive club and a great place to be, because they want to give their young players a chance in the first team."

ENGLAND STAR!

RAHEEM SAYS: "I'm playing for the England Under-18s and I want to work my way up. I've had some enjoyable international highlights so far, like the goal I scored against Rwanda at the Under-17 World Cup, which saw my name trending on Twitter! I want to play in more matches like that."

MEGA FACTPACK!

Full Name: Raheem Shaquille Sterling
Nickname: Razza
Date Of Birth: December 8, 1994
Position: Winger
Club: Liverpool
Country: England
Top Skill: Rapid dribbling

MATCH Tube

STERLING'S SPECIAL SKILLS!
Visit www.youtube.com/matchymovie to watch an awesome skills video from when Sterling met MATCH!

RONALDO

FACTPACK!

Club: Real Madrid
Position: Winger
Age: 27
Height: 6ft 1in
Value: £100 million
Country: Portugal

Did you know? Ronaldo has been named FIFA World Player Of The Year once and finished runner-up twice!

THE BIG QUIZ!

HEAD OF TWO HALVES!

Which two Prem stars have their faces messed up?

5 POINTS FOR EACH CORRECT ANSWER

MY SCORE | 10

TOP HALF...

BOTTOM HALF...

CLUB SHARERS!

Which team have these stars all played for?

10 POINTS FOR THE CORRECT ANSWER

MY SCORE | 10

ONUOHA

ROBINHO

GIVEN

BOATENG

STURRIDGE

5 QUESTIONS ON...

WAYNE ROONEY

1 Before joining Man. United way back in 2004, which Premier League club did Rooney play for?

2 True or False? Wazza has never won the FA Cup!

3 How many Premier League goals did the Man. United legend score in the 2011-12 season – 25, 27 or 29?

4 Against which country did Rooney score his only goal at Euro 2012 – France, Sweden or Ukraine?

5 In what year was the England superstar named PFA Player Of The Year – 2010, 2011 or 2012?

2 POINTS FOR EACH CORRECT ANSWER

MY SCORE | 10

STAR JUMBLE!

Which players' names are scrambled up?

2 POINTS FOR EACH CORRECT ANSWER

MY SCORE | 10

Harden Daze

An Eighth Join

Bandage Lend Her

Market Creepers

Local Ear Curls

WORDFIT!

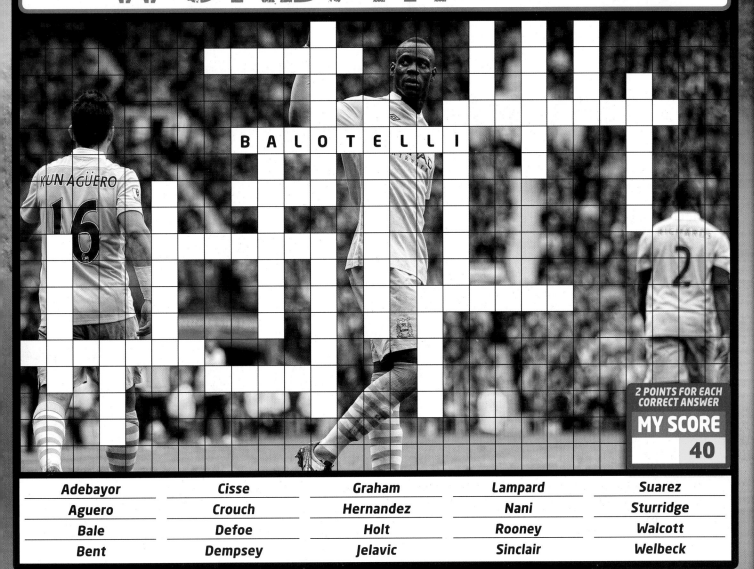

B A L O T E L L I

2 POINTS FOR EACH CORRECT ANSWER

MY SCORE 40

Adebayor	Cisse	Graham	Lampard	Suarez
Aguero	Crouch	Hernandez	Nani	Sturridge
Bale	Defoe	Holt	Rooney	Walcott
Bent	Dempsey	Jelavic	Sinclair	Welbeck

FLASHBACK!

5 POINTS FOR EACH CORRECT ANSWER

MY SCORE 20

Can you name the Real Madrid superstars in these mega ancient photos?

THE MADRID STAR IS...

THE MADRID STAR IS...

THE MADRID STAR IS...

THE MADRID STAR IS...

ANSWERS ON PAGE 92

SPOT THE DIFFERENCE!

Find the ten changes we've made to these Chelsea pics from the FA Cup final!

2012 WINNERS

2011 WINNERS

ANSWERS ON PAGE 92

5 POINTS FOR EACH CORRECT ANSWER

MY SCORE

50

THE AWESOME ADVENTURES OF MATCHMAN

MERRY CHRISTMAS, MATCH FANS! CHECK OUT MATCH EVERY TUESDAY FOR MORE GREAT CARTOONS!

SNAPPED!

BEST OF 2012 SPECIAL!

Yakubu and Ali Al Habsi scrap it out for tonight's chicken dinner!

Dortmund keeper Roman Weidenfeller badly needed that hairwash!

Lamps is happy to finally get rid of those boots!

Stuart Pearce tries to prove he could've played for Team GB at London 2012!

 **Arsenal** **5**

Sagna 40, Van Persie 43, Rosicky 51,
Walcott 65, 68

 **Tottenham** **2**

Saha 4, Adebayor (pen) 34

Date: February 26 **Venue:** Emirates Stadium

Tournament: Premier League

What happened? In an amazing North London derby, Louis Saha and Emmanuel Adebayor blasted Spurs into a two-goal lead, but Arsenal had other ideas! In an incredible half-hour spell, Bacary Sagna pulled one back and Robin van Persie's stunning strike put Arsenal level at half-time, before Tomas Rosicky and a Theo Walcott double completed an unforgettable fightback!

What Do You Remember?

1 Emmanuel Adebayor scored the penalty in this match, but which Spurs winger was fouled in the area by Arsenal's Wojciech Szczesny?

2 Which Tottenham midfielder was sent off for a foul on Thomas Vermaelen late in the game – Luka Modric, Scott Parker or Tom Huddlestone?

3 The Gunners scored five goals against which other London club last season – Chelsea or QPR?

4 Which Tottenham defender started his last ever North London derby in this clash!

5 True or False? Spurs striker Adebayor scored his penalty on his 28th birthday!

ANSWERS: 1. Gareth Bale; **2.** Scott Parker; **3.** Chelsea; **4.** Ledley King; **5.** True.

WORDSEARCH!

Can you find 25 massive European teams hiding in this giant grid?

```
C H E L S E A M Y R N M Q R D A Z I T B
V V A L E N C I A E B A Q S R O A N C E
T A U C T I Y M E I U N P S P L C T A N
Z U U E N E O V K Y Z C Z H V Y M E C F
L B Y H L F N A E O S I I Z Y M I R C I
M K G L J E E E U S E T X A Y P L M E C
J O I E R M M Y U W P Y R U L I A I L A
K L N E T Y T T E V V A D J W A N L T X
F H E T M A N R B N S L N Q Q K S A I E
K H S E P E F A A A O N I Y Q O J N C A
Y Z Z C V E E T B R O A V O S X R C I
B V W U H F L A U Q Z C R P E L Q O C V
R D J A R A L L Q W F O E D O R T M E G
F Q A J M A L P I X M A N L W L P A E S
Y E Q A G K P K M E S X U S O L I O R H
H Y K X U Y V R E V R W J V P N A U O Q
Z V X D N F B C R I Q P O R T O A G K L
B T M W R S R E A L M A D R I D R H O Z
```

AC Milan	Chelsea	Heerenveen	Man. City	Real Madrid
Ajax	Espanyol	Inter Milan	Montpellier	Roma
Barcelona	Feyenoord	Juventus	Napoli	Schalke
Benfica	Galatasaray	Lille	Olympiakos	Trabzonspor
Celtic	Getafe	Liverpool	Porto	Valencia

ANSWERS ON PAGE 92

GERRARD

FACT PACK!

Club: Liverpool

Position: Midfielder

Age: 32

Height: 6ft 1in

Value: £15 million

Country: England

Did you know? Gerrard was the only England player to be named in UEFA's Team Of The Tournament at Euro 2012 last summer!

BOOT SPOTTER!

Check out the best boots the stars were wearing in 2012!

Samir Nasri
Adidas Predator LZ

➡ After months of seeing prototype Predator Lethal Zones, Adidas' awesome power boot hit the world in April!

➡ Adidas revealed each unique zone over five weeks, starting with First Touch on Nasri's white and red boots!

➡ Drive, Pass, Dribble and Sweet Spot were then unveiled before the launch blue, white and infrared version blew us away!

BEST OF THE REST!

Check out these other wicked boot spots!

Cristiano Ronaldo
Nike Mercurial Vapor VIII

➡ Back at the start of 2012, the Real Madrid superstar was spotted wearing CR Mercurial Vapor Superfly IIIs! But these cool Nike speed boots were actually disguised Vapor VIIIs that hit stores in a cool mango and grey colourway in March!

Sergio Aguero
Puma Camo Testing

➡ The Man. City striker is lethal in his class evoSPEED 1 boots, but back in spring Kun was spotted wearing a strange pair of Pumas in training! Only 50 pairs of these limited edition boots were available to buy!

Jon Walters
Stoke
Pantofola d'Oro Lazzarini

Christian Maggio
Italy
Lotto Stadio Potenza Italy II

Hulk
Brazil
Mizuno Morelia Neo

Robert Lewandowski
Poland
Nike T90 Laser IV

THE BIG QUIZ!

JOB SWAP!

Which Prem legend has quit footy to work as a club DJ in this pic?

10 POINTS FOR THE CORRECT ANSWER

MY SCORE
10

NAME THE MANAGER!

Do you know the gaffers of these teams?

2 POINTS FOR EACH CORRECT ANSWER

MY SCORE
10

TOTTENHAM

ASTON VILLA

NORWICH

LIVERPOOL

BARCELONA

5 QUESTIONS ON...

VINCENT KOMPANY

1 Man. City signed the powerful centre-back from which Bundesliga club back in 2008?

2 How old is the tough-tackling City defender – 26, 27 or 28 years old?

3 Which international team does Kompany play for – Belgium, Czech Republic, France or Holland?

4 Which two major trophies has Man. City's captain won since arriving at the Etihad Stadium?

5 Kompany took over as his country's captain from which Arsenal defender last year?

2 POINTS FOR EACH CORRECT ANSWER

MY SCORE
10

WHO AM I?

Can you work out the mystery Premier League star from these three clues?

THE MYSTERY STAR IS...

1 I'm a lethal striker and I joined my current club back in January!

2 I cost £10 million when I moved from German side Freiburg!

3 I scored 13 Premier League goals in just 13 starts last season!

10 POINTS FOR THE CORRECT ANSWER

MY SCORE
10

WORDSEARCH!

Can you find 20 wicked world superstars in this giant grid?

```
F F H X U W S J Z C Z L E W A N D O W S K I C X I C G
A H U L K B K A O E Y J I T S I Z R M I I K M N X V D
Z E X A H U K Z M E F S R D U P F X S G P M C E V J A
X M N W E O H O J E O S T C X O I S G F Q S T Y M B T
R M V M X M G H R I B E R Y O F E R B M B V O M L G V
F A X E J Q B O S Y L R F T N M W O L H U H D A T H I
F V H C F T P P K H P M A Z T Q D L L O F I V R F C P
F U R R B L P U R A J D O C P L F Y V X F D O G A Q O
O I O K C E L P Y P M H B D A K R C W T O U E Z B I B
L C N X A V I U K O F S H N R V E T O R N H E M R B R
E R P I J Y I Z Y J L M O A S I L F W N R H S I E A S
P W H F E J K Z A Q T R W E R I C F M U C I O K G H Z
C E V U L S A Y K H U A D H Z T D U Q N F D I B A O W
M Q G R C E T E A F L E B O X L B D A C F Q G G S H H
V E H Y S K O A G A G U E R O Z W S I W H J S J Z A B
H C A S I L L A S I T C M P F D C D Q A F X L Y B C O
C I N B L M R M J V K Z M H Q A H L Q F W N E F N C U
```

Aguero	Fabregas	Iniesta	Neymar	Ribery
Alba	Gomez	Lewandowski	Ozil	Ronaldo
Buffon	Hart	Messi	Pirlo	Sanchez
Casillas	Hulk	Modric	Puyol	Xavi

FLASHBACK!

Which England players will want to forget these dodgy old pics?

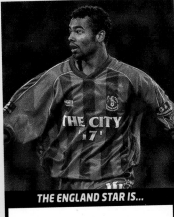

THE ENGLAND STAR IS...

THE ENGLAND STAR IS...

THE ENGLAND STAR IS...

THE ENGLAND STAR IS...

ANSWERS ON PAGE 92

WORLD DREAM TEAM!

Pick your team of the planet's hottest players, and if it's the same as MATCH's you could win some awesome footy prizes!

WORLD DREAM TEAM
GOALKEEPERS!

JOE HART
Club: Man. City ★ **Age:** 25
Country: England ★ **Value:** £25m

England's No.1 was in world-class form in 2012 as Man. City won their first Premier League title! Hart's rapid reflexes, brave saves and clean sheets record earned him his second Golden Glove award in a row!

PETR CECH
Club: Chelsea ★ **Age:** 30
Country: Czech Rep. ★ **Value:** £14m

Chelsea hero Cech was back to his best in 2012! The giant keeper played in his 250th Prem game for The Blues and saved three penalties as Chelsea were crowned champions of Europe for the first time ever!

IKER CASILLAS
Club: Real Madrid ★ **Age:** 31
Country: Spain ★ **Value:** £20m

What a year the legendary keeper had in 2012! Super-cool Casillas captained Real Madrid to their first La Liga title since 2008, and led Spain to Euro 2012 glory with some stunning performances!

GIANLUIGI BUFFON
Club: Juventus ★ **Age:** 34
Country: Italy ★ **Value:** £12m

It's been over ten years since Gigi broke the transfer record for a keeper, and he's still going strong! Juve won the Serie A title and conceded just 20 goals in 2011-12 thanks to Buffon's incredible form!

MANUEL NEUER
Club: Bayern Munich ★ **Age:** 26
Country: Germany ★ **Value:** £25m

Neuer had a fantastic debut season for Bayern! The ice-cool shot-stopper saved penalties from Ronaldo and Kaka in the Champions League semi-final shoot-out, and even scored one himself in the final against Chelsea!

BEST OF THE REST!
CHECK OUT THESE OTHER SUPERSTARS!

DAVID DE GEA
Man. United

HUGO LLORIS
Lyon

PEPE REINA
Liverpool

VICTOR VALDES
Barcelona

NOW PICK YOUR WORLD DREAM TEAM KEEPER!

TURN TO PAGE 36

WORLD DREAM TEAM
CENTRE-BACKS!

SERGIO RAMOS

Club: Real Madrid ★ **Age:** 26

Country: Spain ★ **Value:** £30m

Ramos was pure class after moving from right-back to centre-back last season! He bossed strikers as Real Madrid won La Liga, then teamed up brilliantly alongside Gerard Pique as Spain defended their Euro crown!

JOHN TERRY

Club: Chelsea ★ **Age:** 31

Country: England ★ **Value:** £18m

The Chelsea skipper will never forget 2012! He led The Blues to his fifth FA Cup win, and played a big part in his side's run to the Champions League win - though he missed the final through suspension!

CARLES PUYOL

Club: Barcelona ★ **Age:** 34

Country: Spain ★ **Value:** £7m

Injury cut short Puyol's season and made him miss Euro 2012, but he's still a wicked centre-back! Everyone knows him for his crazy hair, but his leadership and strength make him one of the world's best defenders!

VINCENT KOMPANY

Club: Man. City ★ **Age:** 26

Country: Belgium ★ **Value:** £25m

Kompany proved he's one of the best defenders in the world during City's charge to the title in 2012! He's got bags of pace, reads the game like a legend and times his tackles to perfection!

MATS HUMMELS

Club: B. Dortmund ★ **Age:** 23

Country: Germany ★ **Value:** £22m

Hummels was in great form last season as Dortmund won back-to-back Bundesliga titles and lifted the German Cup! Hummels' organisation, technique and distribution from the back were top class!

BEST OF THE REST!
CHECK OUT THESE OTHER SUPERSTARS!

HOLGER BADSTUBER
Bayern Munich

FABRICIO COLOCCINI
Newcastle

RIO FERDINAND
Man. United

LAURENT KOSCIELNY
Arsenal

JOLEON LESCOTT
Man. City

PEPE

Club: Real Madrid ★ **Age:** 29

Country: Portugal ★ **Value:** £20m

Real Madrid's defence was rock solid in 2012 with Pepe playing alongside Sergio Ramos! The powerful Portugal star's tight man-marking, awesome aerial ability and bone-crunching tackles gave strikers nightmares!

ANDREA BARZAGLI

Club: Juventus ★ **Age:** 31

Country: Italy ★ **Value:** £13m

Barzagli blasted into MATCH's list of centre-backs with loads of awesome displays in 2011-12! He was a regular in Juve's defence that won the Serie A title, and that earned him a recall to Italy's team in time for Euro 2012!

THIAGO SILVA

Club: PSG ★ **Age:** 28

Country: Brazil ★ **Value:** £35m

PSG broke the transfer record for a defender when they signed the Brazil megastar from AC Milan last summer! He's quick, has a top footy brain and will do anything to stop the ball hitting the back of the net!

GIORGIO CHIELLINI

Club: Juventus ★ **Age:** 28

Country: Italy ★ **Value:** £15m

No-nonsense defending is what Chiellini is all about! Whether he was playing at centre-back or full-back last season, the powerful star had strikers in his pocket as Juve beat AC Milan to the Serie A title!

GERARD PIQUE

Club: Barcelona ★ **Age:** 25

Country: Spain ★ **Value:** £30m

The classy centre-back was in mind-blowing form for Barcelona and Spain this year! Pique's strong in the air and hardly ever gets beaten on the ground thanks to his speed, footy brain and well-timed tackles!

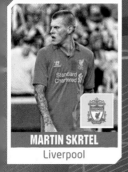

MARTIN SKRTEL
Liverpool

NEVEN SUBOTIC
Borussia Dortmund

THOMAS VERMAELEN
Arsenal

JAN VERTONGHEN
Tottenham

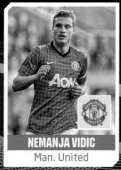

NEMANJA VIDIC
Man. United

NOW PICK YOUR WORLD DREAM TEAM CENTRE-BACKS!

TURN TO PAGE 36

WORLD DREAM TEAM
FULL-BACKS!

PHILIPP LAHM

Club: Bayern Munich ★ **Age:** 28

Country: Germany ★ **Value:** £20m

Lahm missed out on silverware in 2012, but was still one of the best full-backs in Europe! He's destroyed opponents for years with his class crosses and laser-guided passes, and he reads the game like a legend!

JORDI ALBA

Club: Barcelona ★ **Age:** 23

Country: Spain **Value:** £20m

Barça bagged a bargain when they snapped up speedy left-back Alba from Valencia for just £11 million! He was in red-hot form at the Euros, and starred in the back four that conceded just one goal all tournament!

BACARY SAGNA

Club: Arsenal ★ **Age:** 29

Country: France ★ **Value:** £14m

The Gunners ace will want to forget last season after breaking his leg and missing Euro 2012! His pace and stamina mean he can power forward when Arsenal attack, but also boss wingers when he has to defend!

FABIO COENTRAO

Club: Real Madrid ★ **Age:** 24

Country: Portugal ★ **Value:** £24m

Coentrao didn't get as much game time as he would have liked for Real last season, but he won the league title and was named in the Euro 2012 Team Of The Tournament as Portugal reached the semi-finals!

LEIGHTON BAINES

Club: Everton ★ **Age:** 27

Country: England ★ **Value:** £14m

Baines is one of the best attacking left-backs in the world! He can whip in deadly crosses and loves to beat keepers with awesome free-kicks! If it wasn't for Ashley Cole, he'd be England's first-choice left-back!

BEST OF THE REST!
CHECK OUT THESE OTHER SUPERSTARS!

IGNAZIO ABATE
AC Milan

ALVARO ARBELOA
Real Madrid

GAEL CLICHY
Man. City

BRANISLAV IVANOVIC
Chelsea

GLEN JOHNSON
Liverpool

ASHLEY COLE

Club: Chelsea ★ **Age:** 31

Country: England ★ **Value:** £15m

Cole was in blistering form in 2012 and got his hands on another FA Cup and the Champions League trophy! His quality performances for club and country make him one of the greatest full-backs of all time!

PATRICE EVRA

Club: Man. United ★ **Age:** 31

Country: France ★ **Value:** £18m

Evra missed just one league match last season and came within seconds of winning his fifth league title! He's a master at frightening opposition full-backs with his clever movement, rapid acceleration and top crossing!

DANI ALVES

Club: Barcelona ★ **Age:** 29

Country: Brazil ★ **Value:** £25m

Dani Alves may have only won the Copa del Rey in 2012, but he's still one of the hottest full-backs in the world! The Barcelona ace loves to bomb forward - he assisted 16 goals in all competitions last season!

MARCELO

Club: Real Madrid ★ **Age:** 24

Country: Brazil ★ **Value:** £28m

Marcelo has been outstanding for the Spanish champs and kept Fabio Coentrao out of the side for most of last season! The Brazil ace loves to bomb forward, and his link-up play with Ronaldo is out of this world!

MATHIEU DEBUCHY

Club: Lille ★ **Age:** 27

Country: France ★ **Value:** £8m

Debuchy has had an unforgettable year! His cracking displays bombing down the right wing for Lille saw him named in Ligue 1's Team Of The Year and bagged him a call-up to France's squad for Euro 2012!

PHIL JONES
Man. United

LUKASZ PISZCZEK
Borussia Dortmund

MICAH RICHARDS
Man. City

GREGORY VAN DER WIEL
Ajax

KYLE WALKER
Tottenham

NOW PICK YOUR WORLD DREAM TEAM FULL-BACKS!

TURN TO PAGE 36

WORLD DREAM TEAM
MIDFIELDERS!

LUKA MODRIC

Club: Real Madrid ★ **Age:** 27

Country: Croatia ★ **Value:** £30m

The creative king uses his rapid acceleration to burst away from opponents, before setting up quick counter attacks with incredible passing and vision! Luka is the pro at unlocking defences!

FRANK LAMPARD

Club: Chelsea ★ **Age:** 34

Country: England ★ **Value:** £8m

The Blues star used his awesome range of passing, deadly free-kicks and rocket shots to score 16 goals, assist ten more, win the FA Cup and lift the Champions League trophy for the first time in his career!

BASTIAN SCHWEINSTEIGER

Club: Bayern Munich ★ **Age:** 28

Country: Germany ★ **Value:** £25m

Injury kept Schweinsteiger sidelined for a large part of last season, but when he did play he showed his class! He has the strength of a bull, runs all day long, and is great at driving his team-mates forward!

XABI ALONSO

Club: Real Madrid ★ **Age:** 30

Country: Spain ★ **Value:** £18m

Alonso controls the pace of games from midfield, and played a big part in Real's La Liga success last season! He then blew crowds away at Euro 2012, and scored twice in Spain's class win against France!

ANDREA PIRLO

Club: Juventus ★ **Age:** 33

Country: Italy ★ **Value:** £8m

Italy's midfield magician ran the show in 2012 as Juve stormed to glory! Pirlo then tore up Euro 2012 – proving he still had bags of class! No-one will ever forget his cool chipped penalty against England!

BEST OF THE REST!

CHECK OUT THESE OTHER SUPERSTARS!

SERGIO BUSQUETS
Barcelona

DANIELE DE ROSSI
Roma

CESC FABREGAS
Barcelona

SAMI KHEDIRA
Real Madrid

CLAUDIO MARCHISIO
Juventus

ANDRES INIESTA

Club: Barcelona ★ **Age:** 28

Country: Spain ★ **Value:** £80m

Euro 2012's Player Of The Tournament is the brains of Barça and Spain's midfield! His ball control is out of this world, and his expert vision means he can play tons of defence-splitting passes!

MESUT OZIL

Club: Real Madrid ★ **Age:** 23

Country: Germany ★ **Value:** £50m

Ozil was unstoppable in 2011-12! In 40 La Liga and Champo League starts, the silky star assisted 20 goals and scored six times! He carried on that form at Euro 2012 with a goal against Italy and three assists!

STEVEN GERRARD

Club: Liverpool ★ **Age:** 32

Country: England ★ **Value:** £15m

Liverpool's legendary captain played his 400th Premier League match for The Reds in 2012, but that wasn't the only highlight of his year! Stevie G lifted the Carling Cup and was England's star at Euro 2012!

XAVI

Club: Barcelona ★ **Age:** 32

Country: Spain ★ **Value:** £20m

Xavi showed once again why he's one of the greatest midfielders of all time with tons of world-class performances for Barcelona and Spain in 2012! The midfield genius never wastes possession!

YAYA TOURE

Club: Man. City ★ **Age:** 29

Country: Ivory Coast ★ **Value:** £28m

Midfielders don't come much better than Yaya Toure! He's a powerhouse who's almost impossible to knock off the ball! His incredible box-to-box runs and expert finishing was vital in City's historic title win!

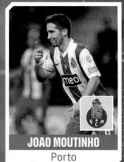

JOAO MOUTINHO
Porto

SCOTT PARKER
Tottenham

PAUL SCHOLES
Man. United

WESLEY SNEIJDER
Inter Milan

ARTURO VIDAL
Juventus

NOW PICK YOUR WORLD DREAM TEAM MIDFIELDERS!

TURN TO PAGE 36

WORLD DREAM TEAM
WINGERS!

ARJEN ROBBEN

Club: Bayern Munich ★ **Age:** 28

Country: Holland ★ **Value:** £25m

Deadly close control and left foot rocket shots are what Robben's game is all about! The Bayern winger ripped the net 12 times in 18 league starts last season, and scored four goals in the Champions League too!

CRISTIANO RONALDO

Club: Real Madrid ★ **Age:** 27

Country: Portugal ★ **Value:** £100m

Ron has been battling it out with Lionel Messi all year to be crowned the best player on the planet! He scored an incredible 60 goals in all comps as Real Madrid won La Liga, before tearing up Euro 2012!

NANI

Club: Man. United ★ **Age:** 25

Country: Portugal ★ **Value:** £26m

Nani guarantees goals and assists with his class technique, vision and rockets shots! The Red Devils skillster has more tricks than a magician, and spends all game delivering precise crosses for United's lethal strikers!

JUAN MATA

Club: Chelsea ★ **Age:** 24

Country: Spain ★ **Value:** £25m

The silky star had a fantastic debut season for the cup double winners in 2011-12! The Blues superstar assisted 13 Premier League goals and scored in the Euro 2012 Final as Spain hammered Italy 4-0!

SAMIR NASRI

Club: Man. City ★ **Age:** 25

Country: France ★ **Value:** £25m

Nasri had an unforgettable season after Roberto Mancini snapped him up from Arsenal! He fed Aguero and Balotelli with killer passes as City won the title, before scoring a cracker against England at Euro 2012!

BEST OF THE REST!

CHECK OUT THESE OTHER SUPERSTARS!

HATEM BEN ARFA
Newcastle

SANTI CAZORLA
Arsenal

ANGEL DI MARIA
Real Madrid

EZEQUIEL LAVEZZI
PSG

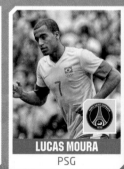

LUCAS MOURA
PSG

GARETH BALE

Club: Tottenham ★ **Age:** 23
Country: Wales ★ **Value:** £40m

With 12 goals and 14 assists in all competitions in 2011-12, Bale's year was sensational! The Wales winger scored more goals in the Prem than ever before and was named in the top flight's Team Of The Season!

EDEN HAZARD

Club: Chelsea ★ **Age:** 21
Country: Belgium ★ **Value:** £32m

Prem defenders need rocket fuel in their boots to keep up with Chelsea new boy Hazard! The Blues busted the bank for the Belgium wonderkid who has rapid pace, lethal dribbling skills and a good eye for goal!

DAVID SILVA

Club: Man. City ★ **Age:** 26
Country: Spain ★ **Value:** £30m

Silva was in electric form for the title winners in 2011-12! He topped the Prem assists chart as City won the title and started every game for Spain in Poland and Ukraine! His goal in the Euro 2012 Final was class!

NENE

Club: PSG ★ **Age:** 31
Country: Brazil ★ **Value:** £10m

Classy winger Nene nearly blasted big-spending PSG to the French title in 2011-12! He topped the Ligue 1 scoring charts with 21 goals, including an incredible 18-minute hat-trick against Rennes!

FRANCK RIBERY

Club: Bayern Munich ★ **Age:** 29
Country: France ★ **Value:** £22m

Ribery was flying in 2012 as Bayern smashed opponents to bits to reach the Champions League final, German Cup final and second place in the Bundesliga! His trickery and mazy dribbles saw him set up 17 goals!

MARCO REUS
Borussia Dortmund

ALEXIS SANCHEZ
Barcelona

ANTONIO VALENCIA
Man. United

THEO WALCOTT
Arsenal

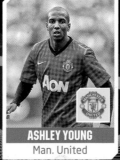

ASHLEY YOUNG
Man. United

NOW PICK YOUR WORLD DREAM TEAM WINGERS!

TURN TO PAGE 36

WORLD DREAM TEAM
STRIKERS!

SERGIO AGUERO
Club: Man. City ★ **Age:** 24

Country: Argentina ★ **Value:** £45m

Aguero didn't stop scoring all season! The Argentina ace hit 23 goals in 31 starts, and sent City fans crazy with his last-gasp goal against QPR to seal the club's first league title in 44 years!

RADAMEL FALCAO
Club: Atletico Madrid ★ **Age:** 26

Country: Colombia ★ **Value:** £45m

Falcao has been linked with a move to the Premier League for ages, and it's easy to see why after he battered defenders in 2012! The lethal hitman scored 24 La Liga goals, and grabbed 12 more in the Europa League!

HULK
Club: Porto ★ **Age:** 26

Country: Brazil ★ **Value:** £35m

Just like the cartoon character Incredible Hulk, the Porto striker uses his strength to destroy anyone in his way! He was named Player Of The Year in Portugal after hitting 16 goals to secure his club's 26th title!

WAYNE ROONEY
Club: Man. United ★ **Age:** 26

Country: England ★ **Value:** £60m

Rooney seemed to score in every game as United nearly won their 20th title! Wazza scored 27 goals in 32 starts in 2011-12, and bagged twice against Liverpool in his 500th career game!

ZLATAN IBRAHIMOVIC
Club: PSG ★ **Age:** 30

Country: Sweden ★ **Value:** £20m

Zlat is the world's most-expensive star in combined transfer fees after moving from AC Milan to PSG last summer! Clubs have spent a crazy £143 million on the Sweden striker during his top career!

BEST OF THE REST!
CHECK OUT THESE OTHER SUPERSTARS!

KARIM BENZEMA
Real Madrid

EDINSON CAVANI
Napoli

PAPISS CISSE
Newcastle

ANTONIO DI NATALE
Udinese

OLIVIER GIROUD
Arsenal

NEYMAR

Club: Santos ★ **Age:** 20

Country: Brazil ★ **Value:** £60m

Neymar has a mad haircut and scored loads of hair-raising goals in 2012! The Brazil superstar netted his 100th career goal back in February, and is the reigning South American Footballer Of The Year!

MARIO BALOTELLI

Club: Man. City ★ **Age:** 22

Country: Italy ★ **Value:** £30m

Love him or hate him, Super Mario is one of the hottest goal machines in the world! The City hero scored 13 times in just 14 starts for the Prem champions, and then had an unbelievable Euro 2012!

ROBIN VAN PERSIE

Club: Man. United ★ **Age:** 29

Country: Holland ★ **Value:** £24m

RVP forgot all about his injury problems in previous seasons to win the Premier League Golden Boot for the first time in 2012! He smashed in 30 goals in 37 games to secure a big-money move to The Red Devils!

LIONEL MESSI

Club: Barcelona ★ **Age:** 25

Country: Argentina ★ **Value:** £120m

The three-time World Player Of The Year had another massive year at Barça! Leo scored an incredible 73 goals in all competitions, including a record 14 in the Champions League! Is he the best player ever?

MARIO GOMEZ

Club: Bayern Munich ★ **Age:** 27

Country: Germany ★ **Value:** £35m

Strong in the air and deadly with both feet, Gomez unleashed goals from all angles in 2012! The hitman scored 26 league goals last season, and was second only to Messi in the Champions League with 12 strikes!

KLAAS-JAN HUNTELAAR
Schalke

ROBERT LEWANDOWSKI
Borussia Dortmund

LUIS SUAREZ
Liverpool

CARLOS TEVEZ
Man. City

FERNANDO TORRES
Chelsea

NOW PICK YOUR WORLD DREAM TEAM STRIKERS!

TURN TO PAGE 36

WORLD DREAM TEAM
MY BEST STARTING XI!

You've seen MATCH's pick of the planet's best players, now pick you favourite starting XI!

GOALKEEPER
David de GEA

RIGHT-BACK

CENTRE-BACK
John Terry

CENTRE-BACK
Carles Puyol

LEFT-BACK

RIGHT WINGER

MIDFIELDER

MIDFIELDER

LEFT WINGER

STRIKER

STRIKER

FACTPACK!

Club: Man. City
Position: Striker
Age: 24
Height: 5ft 7ins
Value: £45 million
Country: Argentina
Did you know? Aguero scored the final goal of the 2011-12 season to seal City's first league title since 1968!

AGUERO

THE BIG QUIZ!

FLASHBACK!

Which Premier League manager looked like this in his playing days?

THE PREM MANAGER IS...

10 POINTS FOR THE CORRECT ANSWER

MY SCORE

10

5 QUESTIONS ON...

FERNANDO TORRES

1 How old is the awesome Chelsea striker - 28, 29 or 30 years old?

2 True or False? Torres started his awesome footy career with La Liga giants Athletic Bilbao!

3 Which Prem club did Torres join before moving to Chelsea in 2011 - Liverpool or Man. United?

4 Torres scored his first Chelsea hat-trick against which London club at the end of last season - QPR, Arsenal, Tottenham or Fulham?

5 How many goals did Torres score for Spain to win the Euro 2012 Golden Boot - two, three, four or five?

2 POINTS FOR EACH CORRECT ANSWER

MY SCORE

10

MISSING PLAYERS!

Fill in the gaps in Spain's team that started the Euro 2012 Final!

Goalkeeper
GK. Iker Casillas

Defenders
RB. Alvaro Arbeloa
CB. Gerard Pique
CB. Sergio Ramos
LB. Jordi Alba

Midfielders
DM. Sergio Busquets
DM. Xabi Alonso
AM. ....

Forwards
FW. David Silva
FW. ....
FW. Andres Iniesta

5 POINTS FOR EACH CORRECT ANSWER

MY SCORE

10

STAR JUMBLE!

Which players' names are scrambled up?

2 POINTS FOR EACH CORRECT ANSWER

MY SCORE

10

Chill Lint

Drain Churned

Arctic Tonsils

Raccoon Tell

Armada Chile

WORDFIT!

RONALDO

2 POINTS FOR EACH CORRECT ANSWER

MY SCORE 40

Alonso	Doumbia	Ibrahimovic	Marchisio	Sneijder
Bale	Falcao	Kagawa	Nene	Toure
Cole	Gerrard	Kompany	Parker	Valencia
Dempsey	Higuain	Lahm	Robben	Walker

CAMERA SHY!

5 POINTS FOR EACH CORRECT ANSWER

MY SCORE 20

Which footy stars are hiding from the MATCH snapper?

Man. United   4

Rooney 41, 69, Welbeck 57, Nani 60

Everton   4

Jelavic 33, 83, Fellaini 67, Pienaar 85

Date: April 22 **Venue:** Old Trafford

Tournament: Premier League

What happened? With less than a month to go until the end of the Premier League season, this epic draw at Old Trafford blew the title race wide open! The Red Devils looked to have wrapped up the points as they raced into a 4-2 lead, but they threw it away in the last seven minutes as Everton scored twice in a crazy three-minute spell to snatch a point!

What Do You Remember?

1 Steven Pienaar was on loan at Everton from which Premier League team last season?

2 Nikica Jelavic joined The Toffees from which famous Scottish club last season?

3 True or False? Wayne Rooney's quality double against his old team in this match made him Man. United's fourth highest goalscorer ever!

4 Marouane Fellaini scored Everton's second goal of the game, but which international team does the giant midfielder play for?

5 Paul Scholes started in midfield in this match, but which England player replaced him late on?

ANSWERS: 1. Tottenham; 2. Rangers; 3. True; 4. Belgium; 5. Phil Jones.

WORDFIT!

Can you fit 25 awesome wingers into this massive grid?

YOUNG

2 POINTS FOR EACH CORRECT ANSWER

MY SCORE

50

BALE	HAZARD	MILNER	RIBERY	SINCLAIR
BEN ARFA	LARSSON	MOSES	ROBBEN	VALENCIA
DI MARIA	LENNON	NANI	RONALDO	WALCOTT
DUFF	MATA	NASRI	SANCHEZ	WILLIAN
GUTIERREZ	McCLEAN	PIENAAR	SILVA	YARMOLENKO

ANSWERS ON PAGE 92

CAZORLA

FACT PACK!

Club: Arsenal

Position: Attacking midfielder

Age: 27

Height: 5ft 6ins

Value: £20 million

Country: Spain

Did you know? The little playmaker won Spain's Player Of The Year award in 2007!

TOP 10 CELEBRATIONS!

Check out the best celebrations from the past 12 months!

NICKLAS BENDTNER

10

The Denmark goal machine scored against Portugal in June and revealed a pair of pants sponsored by a betting company! He was fined £80,000 because it's against UEFA rules!

9

THEO WALCOTT

The England winger came off the bench and buried England's equaliser against Sweden at the Euros! Theo was so shocked, he just stood there and shrugged!

DIDIER DROGBA

8

Stamford Bridge went mental when Drog put Chelsea ahead against Barça in the Champo League semi-final! He ran to the corner flag, slid on his knees and saluted The Blues' fans!

7

WAYNE ROONEY

After returning from suspension against Ukraine at Euro 2012, Wazza bagged the winner and pretended to spray his hair! Why? Because Andy Carroll had lent him his hair product before the match!

GARETH BALE

6

Tottenham's wing wizard honoured late Wales boss Gary Speed when he scored against Bolton last season! He removed his boots to reveal 'RIP Gary Speed' written on them!

5 — EMMANUEL ADEBAYOR

Ade busted out some top moves when he ripped the net during his loan spell at Spurs last season, and he even teamed up with Bale after his goal against Norwich! Maybe he should enter Strictly Come Dancing?

4 — MARIO BALOTELLI

After blasting two goals past Germany in the Euro 2012 semi-finals, Super Mario ripped off his shirt and showed off his massive guns! You don't want to mess with the Italy striker!

2 — GARY NEVILLE

aaargghhh... unbelievable!

The Sky Sports commentator lost it when Fernando Torres scored against Barça to put Chelsea into the Champions League final! We'll never forget the noise he made!

3 — CRISTIANO RONALDO

Ron and Messi battled it out for goals all year, so the Portugal legend couldn't resist sending Leo a message from Euro 2012! He blew the Barça ace a kiss after his goal in the quarter-finals against the Czech Republic!

1 — NEYMAR & MARCELO

Brazil turned on the Samba style at London 2012, and one of the highlights was Neymar's cool celebration against Belarus! He pulled out Usain Bolt's lightning pose with team-mate Marcelo!

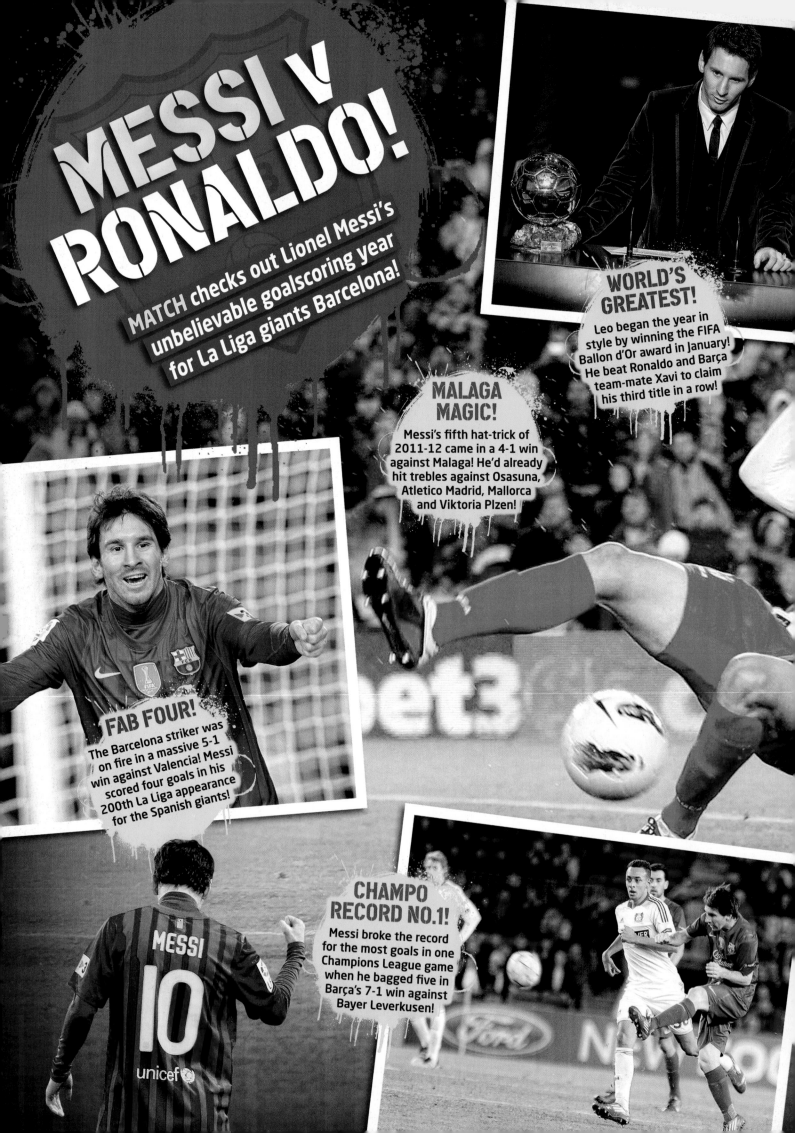

MESSI V RONALDO!

MATCH checks out Lionel Messi's unbelievable goalscoring year for La Liga giants Barcelona!

WORLD'S GREATEST!

Leo began the year in style by winning the FIFA Ballon d'Or award in January! He beat Ronaldo and Barça team-mate Xavi to claim his third title in a row!

MALAGA MAGIC!

Messi's fifth hat-trick of 2011-12 came in a 4-1 win against Malaga! He'd already hit trebles against Osasuna, Atletico Madrid, Mallorca and Viktoria Plzen!

FAB FOUR!

The Barcelona striker was on fire in a massive 5-1 win against Valencia! Messi scored four goals in his 200th La Liga appearance for the Spanish giants!

CHAMPO RECORD NO.1!

Messi broke the record for the most goals in one Champions League game when he bagged five in Barça's 7-1 win against Bayer Leverkusen!

MESSI 10

unicef

GREAT AGAINST GRANADA!

Another record fell in March after Leo hit a treble against Granada! It made him Barça's highest ever goalscorer and broke a 55-year-old record!

CHAMPO RECORD NO.2!

Leo equalled the Champo League record of 14 goals in one season at the start of April, when he netted twice against AC Milan from the penalty spot!

KING OF EUROPE!

Messi bagged another hat-trick against Malaga in May! His stunning treble made him the highest goalscorer in a single European season!

CUP WINNER!

Messi finished his record-shattering season with his 73rd goal in all comps against Athletic Bilbao in the Copa del Rey final! He assisted 23 goals, too!

DERBY DESTROYER!

Three days after his treble against Malaga, Messi scored every goal in a 4-0 win over city rivals Espanyol! It took his total to a mind-blowing 72 goals in all comps!

MESSI V RONALDO!

MATCH takes a closer look at Cristiano Ronaldo's awesome net busting year for Real Madrid!

SUPER SECOND!
Ronaldo kicked off his year with the FIFA Ballon d'Or runners-up spot! He saw off Barça megastar Xavi, but couldn't beat Messi to the top prize!

BARÇA'S BOGEYMAN!
Ronaldo loved playing against Barcelona last season! He scored twice against them in the Copa del Rey, before bagging at the Nou Camp to all but seal the Spanish title for Real!

TREBLE TIME!
Ron scored his sixth La Liga hat-trick of 2011-12 against Levante in February! He scored a world-class backheel against Rayo Vallecano that month, too!

SWEET CENTURY!
When the Portugal ace netted twice against Real Sociedad at the end of March, he became the fastest player ever to score 100 La Liga goals!

TOP TEN!

Despite losing on pens in the Champions League semi-final, Ron still scored twice against Bayern! He finished the competition's third-highest scorer behind Mario Gomez and Messi with ten goals!

FAB FORTY!

Ronaldo scored his 40th league goal of the season against city rivals Atletico! It was the second season in a row that he'd ripped the net that many times!

TABLE TOPPERS!

In the last game of the season, Ronaldo scored his 46th league goal! It meant he'd scored against every La Liga team in 2011-12 as Real won the title!

SUPER SIXTY!

Ronaldo finished his third season at the Bernabeu with a jaw-dropping 60 goals and 15 assists in all competitions! He's one of the greatest players on the planet!

AWESOME AWARD!

Before heading to Euro 2012, Ron became the first Real Madrid star since Raul in 2008 to win the Alfredo di Stefano Trophy as the best player in La Liga!

HOW THEY SCORED THEIR GOALS IN 2011-12!

HEAD
Messi: 3
Ronaldo: 7

LEFT FOOT
Messi: 60
Ronaldo: 10

RIGHT FOOT
Messi: 10
Ronaldo: 43

PENALTIES
Messi: 14
Ronaldo: 14

HAT-TRICKS
Messi: 10
Ronaldo: 7

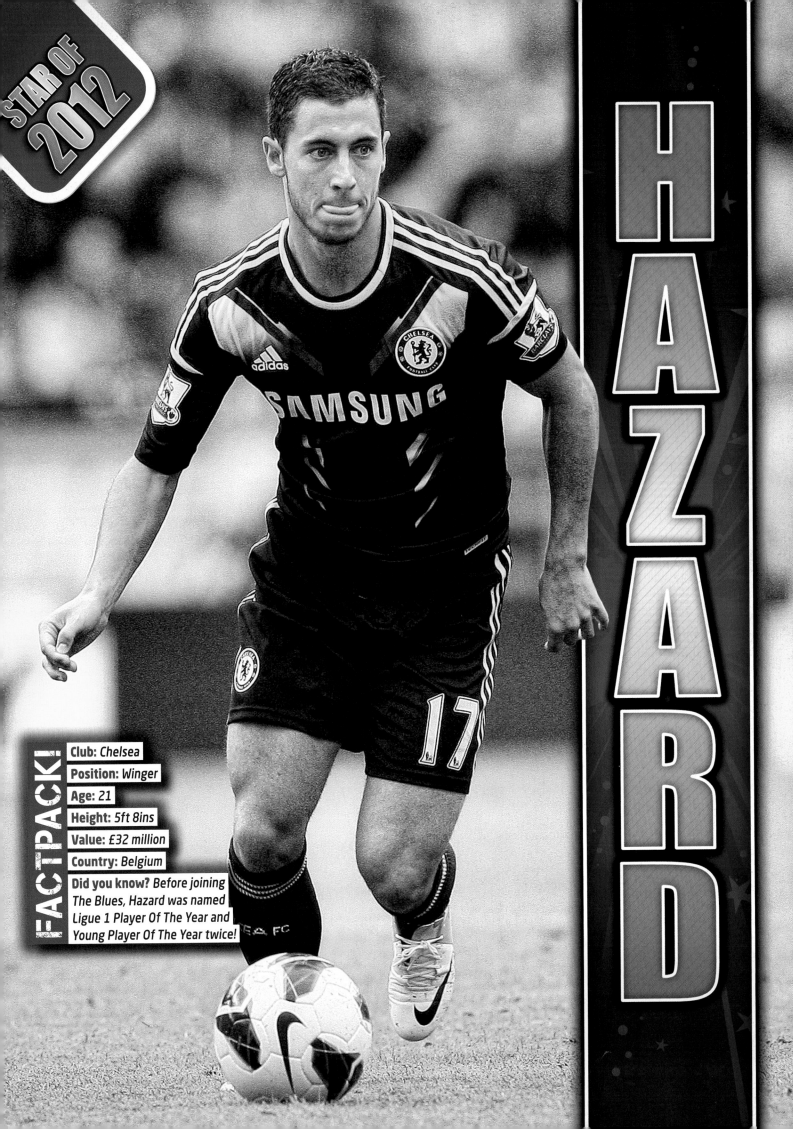

STAR OF 2012

HAZARD

 **Barcelona** **2**

Busquets 35, Iniesta 43

 **Chelsea** **2**

Ramires 45, Torres 90

Date: April 24 **Venue:** Nou Camp

Tournament: Champions League

What happened? Despite holding a 1-0 lead from the first leg, no-one gave Chelsea a chance at the Nou Camp! Sergio Busquets' opener, John Terry's red card and Andres Iniesta's finish looked to have ended The Blues' Champions League dreams before half-time! But they defended like legends, and reached the final after Ramires scored a world-class chip and Torres raced clear to slot home their second in stoppage-time!

What Do You Remember?

1 Which Chelsea defender went off injured after just 12 minutes in this massive clash – Branislav Ivanovic, Gary Cahill or Ashley Cole?

2 Which Barcelona megastar hit the crossbar from the penalty spot in the second half?

3 Who was Chelsea's manager in this match – Roberto di Matteo or Andre Villas-Boas?

4 Blues captain John Terry was shown a red card for fouling which Barcelona forward?

5 Who scored the only goal of the game in the Champions League semi-final first leg at Stamford Bridge – Didier Drogba or Frank Lampard?

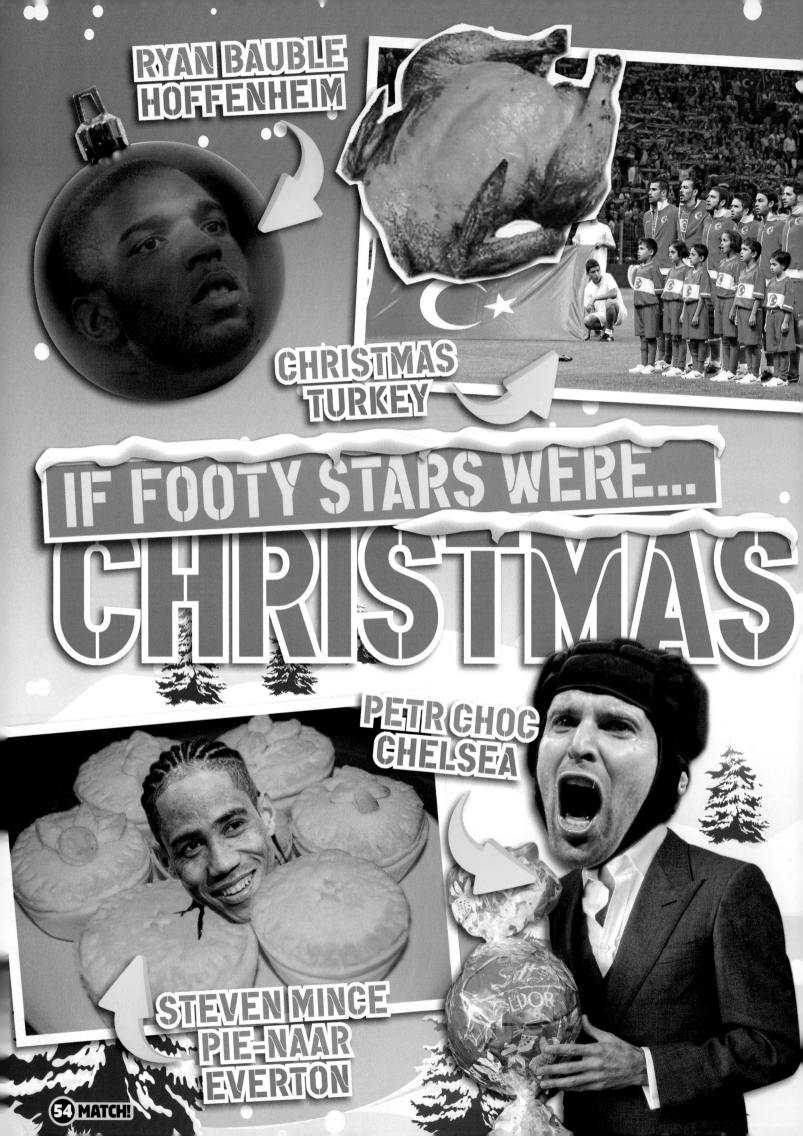

RYAN BAUBLE
HOFFENHEIM

CHRISTMAS
TURKEY

IF FOOTY STARS WERE...
CHRISTMAS

PETR CHOC
CHELSEA

STEVEN MINCE
PIE-NAAR
EVERTON

PER MERTE-
CRACKER
ARSENAL

DIRK SPROUT
FENERBAHCE

THINGS!

SANTA
CAZORLA
ARSENAL

ARJEN ROBIN
B. MUNICH

IAN HOLLY-WAY
BLACKPOOL

ROONEY

FACTPACK!

Club: Man. United
Position: Striker
Age: 26
Height: 5ft 10ins
Value: £60 million
Country: England

Did you know? Rooney has scored more Champo League goals than any other English player! He overtook Paul Scholes' record last year!

THE BEST BITS OF...
EURO 2

MEGA MATCHES!

Sweden 2-3 England

The Three Lions battled back from 2-1 down to beat Sweden in Group D! Theo Walcott came off the bench to score a long-ranger, before setting up Danny Welbeck who flicked home the winner!

Germany 4-2 Greece

Georgios Samaras shocked Germany when he made it 1-1 in the second half, but Joachim Low's side turned on the style to reach the semi-finals! Lahm, Khedira, Klose and Reus' goals rocked!

Denmark 2-3 Portugal

It was end-to-end stuff in Lviv, as Nicklas Bendtner's double cancelled out Portugal's two-goal lead! Super sub Silvestre Varela was having none of it though, as he smashed in a late winner!

Spain 1-1 Italy

Spain looked in trouble when Antonio di Natale put Italy ahead, but Del Bosque's side pulled level four minutes later when Cesc Fabregas fired home – the midfielder was playing as a striker!

O12!

MATCH looks back at the best goals, games, fans and more from Poland and Ukraine last summer!

UEFA EURO 2012

NET BUSTERS!

Zlat's Volley!

The best goal of Euro 2012 came in Sweden's last match against France! Zlatan Ibrahimovic's awesome volley flew past Hugo Lloris, meaning England topped the group!

Pirlo's Penalty!

Italy's creative king showed his class in the quarter-final penalty shoot-out against England! Joe Hart thought Pirlo was going to put it in the corner, but he chipped it coolly down the middle!

Carroll's Cracker!

The powerful England striker used his incredible aerial strength to put The Three Lions ahead against Sweden! Carroll got on the end of Steven Gerrard's long ball to score an unstoppable header!

Kuba's Belter!

Poland captain Jakub Blaszczykowski sent Warsaw wild with a stunning left-footed strike that flew past Vyacheslav Malafeev in Russia's goal! It was one of the best strikes of the tournament!

CRAZY FANS!

ENGLAND

HOLLAND

ITALY

GREECE

ENGLAND & IRELAND!

Roy's Boys!

Everyone thought Harry Redknapp would get the England job, but it was given to Roy Hodgson! He called up young stars The Ox, Jack Butland, Jordan Henderson and Martin Kelly!

Group Winners!

The Three Lions drew 1-1 with France in their opener, but beat Sweden and Ukraine to finish top of Group D! But there was major heartbreak in the quarter-finals as England lost 4-2 on penalties to Italy!

Home Early!

Republic Of Ireland were drawn in a tough group! Sean St. Ledger gave Ireland hope against Croatia, but goals from Mandzukic and Jelavic stole the points! They then fell apart against Spain and Italy!

Fab Fans!

Thousands of Republic Of Ireland fans sang their hearts out for Giovanni Trapattoni's team! Even though they returned home without a single point, they had a party they'll never forget at Euro 2012!

CRAZY MOMENTS!

Mad Cuts!
Greasy ponytails were everywhere! Andy Carroll, Federico Balzaretti and Zlatan Ibrahimovic loved them! Wazza's hair had a shocker, and Bruno Alves' barnet didn't know what it was doing for Portugal!

Super Shocks!
Holland were one of the faves to win Euro 2012, but they were dumped out with no points! In Group A, no-one gave Greece and the Czech Republic a chance, but they went through instead of Russia and Poland!

Guess The Score!
After Paul The Octopus at World Cup 2012, animal psychics loved predicting results at the Euros! Citta the elephant, Funtik the pig and even a ferret called Fred became megastars! That's crazy!

STARS OF THE EUROS!

Alan Dzagoev
The 22-year-old star scored three goals at the Euros! Two came in Russia's first match against Czech Republic!

Mario Mandzukic
The Croatia forward made a massive impact! He scored twice against Ireland and another against Italy!

Cristiano Ronaldo
The Real Madrid winger was super slick at the Euros! Ronaldo led Portugal all the way to the semi-finals!

Steven Gerrard
England's captain assisted three goals for Roy Hodgson's side! His crosses for Carroll and Lescott's goals were class!

Andrea Pirlo
Footy experts thought the Italy legend was finished, but he turned on the style with loads of quality displays!

Mario Gomez
The Germany striker finally took his domestic club form onto the big stage with three goals in Poland and Ukraine!

Andres Iniesta
The silky playmaker won the Player Of The Tournament after running Spain's midfield on their march to glory!

Mario Balotelli
The Italy ace blew sides away with his finishing! MATCH will never forget his stunning double against Germany!

SPAIN WI

Silva celebrates the opening goal in the Euro final

Mata thanks team-mate Torres for his epic assist

El Nino won the Golden Boot with three goals

N AGAIN!

SPAIN HAMMER ITALY IN THE EURO 2012 FINAL

Reigning champions Spain became the first team to win two European Championships in a row as they thrashed Italy 4-0 in Kiev! David Silva's header opened the scoring, and Jordi Alba added another before half-time as he made a run from his own half! Fernando Torres came off the bench to score Spain's third and then set up Juan Mata late in the game! That meant Torres also won the Golden Boot!

Alba was one of the stars of the tournament

Spain's stars pose with the famous Euro trophy

THE BIG QUIZ!

HEAD OF TWO HALVES!

Which Prem legends have their heads mashed together?

5 POINTS FOR EACH CORRECT ANSWER

MY SCORE 10

TOP HALF...

BOTTOM HALF...

BOGUS BADGES!

Which clubs do these badges belong to?

2 POINTS FOR EACH CORRECT ANSWER

MY SCORE 10

1.

2.

3.

4.

5.

5 QUESTIONS ON...

GARETH BALE

1 In which Welsh city was Bale born - Bangor, Swansea or Cardiff?

2 How old is the world-class Tottenham and Wales winger - 21, 22 or 23 years old?

3 Bale has played for Spurs and which other Premier League club - Southampton or Stoke?

4 True or False? The electric winger played for Team GB at the London 2012 Olympic Games!

5 Which super-cool Adidas boots does Gareth wear - Predator Lethal Zones, F50 adiZeros, adiPURE 11Pros or Copa Mundials?

2 POINTS FOR EACH CORRECT ANSWER

MY SCORE 10

WHO AM I?

Can you work out the mystery Premier League star from these three clues?

THE MYSTERY STAR IS...

1 I'm 27 years old and play in defence for a massive London club!

2 I joined my Prem side from French club Lorient back in 2010!

3 I play international footy for France and made one start at Euro 2012!

10 POINTS FOR THE CORRECT ANSWER

MY SCORE 10

WORDFIT!

Fit all of these Spanish footy stars into the massive grid below!

I N I E S T A

2 POINTS FOR EACH CORRECT ANSWER

MY SCORE 40

Alba	Casillas	Martinez	Puyol	Thiago
Alonso	De Gea	Mata	Ramos	Torres
Arbeloa	Fabregas	Muniain	Reina	Valdes
Busquets	Llorente	Pique	Silva	Xavi

EURO GIANTS!

Which European countries do these massive teams play in?

4 POINTS FOR EACH CORRECT ANSWER

MY SCORE 20

| Basel | Nordsjaelland | Malaga | Braga | Anzhi |

ANSWERS ON PAGE 92

 Man. City `3`

Zabaleta 39, Dzeko 90+2, Aguero 90+5

 QPR `2`

Cisse 48, Mackie 66

Date: May 13 **Venue:** Etihad Stadium

Tournament: Premier League

What happened? In the most nerve-shredding finish to a Premier League season of all time, Man. City beat rivals Man. United to the title on goal difference! City looked to have blown it as they trailed QPR 2-1 when the match went into injury time, but Edin Dzeko pulled City level and Sergio Aguero lifted the roof off the Etihad with a winner seconds from the final whistle!

What Do You Remember?

1 Which QPR midfielder was sent off in this incredible match - Joey Barton, Shaun Wright-Phillips, Adel Taarabt or Shaun Derry?

2 How many years had it been since Man. City last won the league title - 22, 33 or 44 years?

3 How many different teams have now won the Premier League since 1992-93 - four or five?

4 Edin Dzeko plays for which international team - Serbia, Bosnia-Herzegovina or Montenegro?

5 Man. United almost beat rivals Man. City to the title last season, but can you remember which team they beat on the last day?

MATCH'S PREM SC[ORE]

MATCH checks out the greatest moments since the Premier League began!

FIRST GOAL!

On August 15, 1992, giant Sheffield United striker Brian Deane headed home the Prem's first-ever goal against Man. United!

MAGIC MATT!

Southampton legend Matt Le Tissier scored an all-time classic Prem goal against Newcastle in 1993! He used some top tricks to ghost past two defenders before slotting past the keeper!

EVERTON'S GREAT ESCAPE!

Everton needed a final-day win in the 1994 season or they'd get relegated! They were two goals down against Wimbledon, but battled back to win 3-2!

JURGEN'S DIVE!

Germany star Jurgen Klinsmann spent the 1994-95 season at Spurs! He scored on his debut against Sheffield Wednesday, and celebrated with a dive on the turf!

TOP TREBLE!

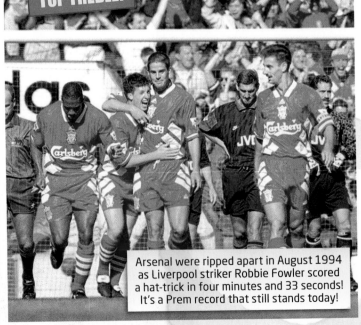

Arsenal were ripped apart in August 1994 as Liverpool striker Robbie Fowler scored a hat-trick in four minutes and 33 seconds! It's a Prem record that still stands today!

RAPBOOK!

After a red card against Crystal Palace in January 1995, Man. United legend Eric Cantona kung-fu kicked a fan as he walked down the tunnel! He picked up an eight-month ban!

UNITED HIT NINE!

The Prem's biggest-ever win was in 1995 when Man. United beat Ipswich 9-0! Andy Cole scored five, Mark Hughes hit two, and Roy Keane and Paul Ince added the others!

KEEGAN'S RANT!

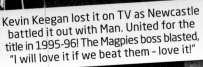

Kevin Keegan lost it on TV as Newcastle battled it out with Man. United for the title in 1995-96! The Magpies boss blasted, "I will love it if we beat them – love it!"

SEVEN-GOAL THRILLER!

During the 1995-96 title run-in, Liverpool beat Newcastle 4-3! Reds striker Stan Collymore bagged an injury-time winner in a Prem classic!

SPLASH THE CASH!

Newcastle smashed the British transfer record when they signed England striker Alan Shearer from Blackburn for £15 million in 1996!

PREM TITLE WINNERS!

Check out who's won the Prem title since 1992-93!

MAN. UNITED – 1992-93

MAN. UNITED – 1993-94

BLACKBURN – 1994-95

MAN. UNITED – 1995-96

MAN. UNITED – 1996-97

PREM SCRAPBOOK!

BECKS' BEAUTY!

David Beckham scored a class goal against Wimbledon back in August 1996! The Man. United ace beat Dons goalkeeper Neil Sullivan from his own half!

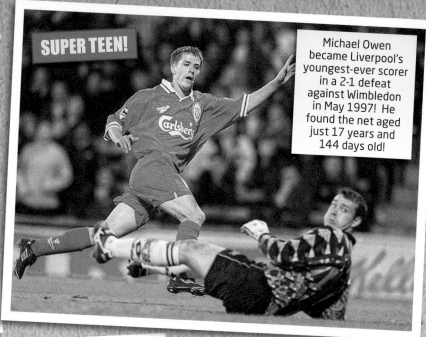

SUPER TEEN!

Michael Owen became Liverpool's youngest-ever scorer in a 2-1 defeat against Wimbledon in May 1997! He found the net aged just 17 years and 144 days old!

REF RAGE!

Former Sheffield Wednesday striker Paolo di Canio went mental with ref Paul Alcock when he was sent off against Arsenal in 1998! He was so angry that he shoved Alcock to the ground!

AL'S HIGH-FIVE!

Alan Shearer never stopped scoring in a Newcastle shirt, and in one game against Sheffield Wednesday in 1999 he was on fire! Big Al scored five goals in a massive 8-0 win at St. James' Park!

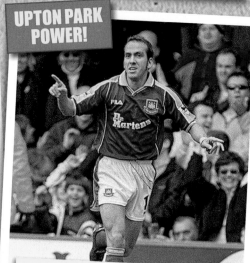

UPTON PARK POWER!

Great Premier League volleys don't come much better than Paolo di Canio's unbelievable scissor-kick against Wimbledon at Upton Park in 2000! It was voted Goal Of The Season!

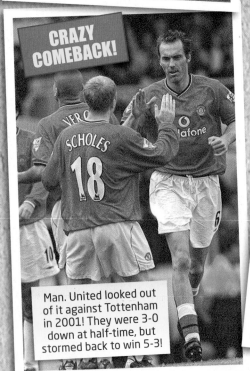

CRAZY COMEBACK!

Man. United looked out of it against Tottenham in 2001! They were 3-0 down at half-time, but stormed back to win 5-3!

DEADLY DENNIS!

Arsenal fans will never forget Dennis Bergkamp's goal against Newcastle in 2002! The Dutch master turned Toon defender Nikos Dabizas inside out before side-footing past Shay Given!

ENK'S OWN-GOAL!

In a game against Birmingham in 2002, Aston Villa keeper Peter Enckelman failed to control an Olof Mellberg throw-in and let the ball slip under his foot and into the net!

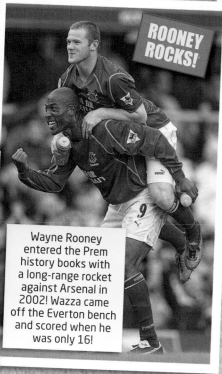

ROONEY ROCKS!

Wayne Rooney entered the Prem history books with a long-range rocket against Arsenal in 2002! Wazza came off the Everton bench and scored when he was only 16!

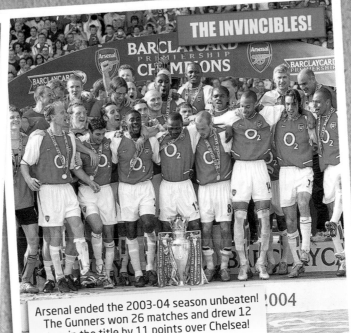

THE INVINCIBLES!

Arsenal ended the 2003-04 season unbeaten! The Gunners won 26 matches and drew 12 to win the title by 11 points over Chelsea!

NEW BOSSES!

Two memorable Prem bosses arrived in England in June 2004! Chelsea hired Jose Mourinho from Porto and Rafa Benitez took over at Liverpool!

MENDES' GHOST GOAL!

In 2005, Man. United keeper Roy Carroll bundled Spurs' Pedro Mendes' long shot way over the line, but the goal wasn't given!

CANARIES CALL!

TV chef Delia Smith tried to get Norwich fans pumped up against Man. City in 2005! She grabbed the mic and shouted, "Where are you? Let's be 'avin' you!"

MAGPIES MASH-UP!

Newcastle team-mates Kieron Dyer and Lee Bowyer were given their marching orders against Aston Villa in 2005! After going 3-0 down, the pair had a massive punch-up!

SUPER SHEARER!

In his final season for Newcastle, Alan Shearer beat a 49-year-old club record when he scored his 201st league goal against Portsmouth at St. James' Park! He retired with 206 goals for The Magpies!

ARSENAL – 1997-98

MAN. UNITED – 1998-99

MAN. UNITED – 1999-2000

MAN. UNITED – 2000-01

ARSENAL – 2001-02

MAN. UNITED – 2002-03

ARSENAL – 2003-04

CHELSEA – 2004-05

PREM SCRAPBOOK!

MEGA TRANSFERS!

There were some crazy signings in 2006! Chelsea paid £30.8 million for AC Milan striker Andrey Shevchenko, and West Ham shocked the footy world by landing Carlos Tevez and Javier Mascherano!

RON AT THE DOUBLE!

Cristiano Ronaldo was unstoppable in 2006-07! He bagged the PFA Player and Young Player Of The Year awards after grabbing 17 goals and 14 assists for Prem champions Man. United!

11-GOAL THRILLER!

Benjani hit a hat-trick for Portsmouth in a stunning match against Reading at Fratton Park in 2007! There were nine different scorers as Pompey won 7-4!

BYE-BYE JOSE!

After winning six trophies in three seasons at Chelsea, Jose Mourinho left the club in September 2007! Avram Grant took over and led The Blues to the Champions League final!

DERBY DESTROYED!

YET ANOTHER RECORD BREAKING SEASON FOR THE RAMS

Derby finished bottom of the Premier League in 2007-08 with just 11 points after managing just one win all season! The Rams have never returned to the top flight since!

DEADLINE-DAY MAYHEM!

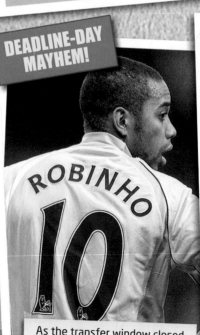

As the transfer window closed in September 2008, Man. City smashed the British transfer record with a £32.5 million move for Real Madrid star Robinho!

AWESOME ANDREY!

Liverpool's 4-4 draw with Arsenal at Anfield in 2009 ruined their chance of winning the title! Andrey Arshavin hit all four Gunners goals in a classic!

WORLD-RECORD TRANSFER!

After six awesome seasons at Old Trafford, Cristiano Ronaldo left Man. United in a record-breaking transfer! Real Madrid paid £80 million for the Portugal winger!

BEACH BALL BONKERS!

MATCH will never forget Sunderland's 1-0 win over Liverpool in 2009! Black Cats striker Darren Bent hit the winner, but his shot deflected off a beach ball before flying past Pepe Reina!

MEGA MOVES!

Cash was flying all over the place in January 2011! Liverpool signed Andy Carroll for £35 million from Newcastle, and Chelsea bought Fernando Torres for £50 million!

MAGPIES MAGIC!

In 2011, Newcastle came back from 4-0 down against Arsenal to draw 4-4! Cheick Tiote's stunning late volley sent the home fans wild!

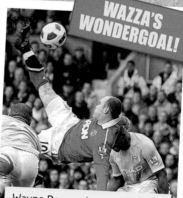

WAZZA'S WONDERGOAL!

Wayne Rooney has scored loads of volleys in his career, but none have topped his winner against rivals Man. City in Man. United's 2010-11 title-winning season!

UNITED'S GREAT EIGHT!

Arsenal suffered their worst defeat since 1896 when Man. United stuffed them 8-2 last season! Ashley Young bagged a double and Wayne Rooney scored an unforgettable hat-trick!

MANCHESTER MAYHEM!

Man. United beat Man. City 4-3 in 2009, but the seven-goal thriller the Manchester giants played out in 2011 was a bit more one-sided! City ripped Fergie's side to pieces in a massive 6-1 win!

CHELSEA – 2005-06

MAN. UNITED – 2006-07

MAN. UNITED – 2007-08

MAN. UNITED – 2008-09

CHELSEA – 2009-10

MAN. UNITED – 2010-11

MAN. CITY – 2011-12

HAVE YOUR SAY!

Who do you think will win the Prem title in 2012-13? Have your say right now on MATCH's Facebook and Twitter pages!

THE BIG QUIZ!

JOB SWAP!

Which Prem star has quit football to work as a teacher in this pic?

10 POINTS FOR THE CORRECT ANSWER

MY SCORE **10**

sagna's MAKEOVER!

THE HIDDEN STAR IS...

10 POINTS FOR THE CORRECT ANSWER

MY SCORE **10**

5 QUESTIONS ON...

DAVID SILVA

1 Which massive La Liga club did Silva play for between 2006 and 2010 – Barcelona, Real Madrid, Valencia or Atletico Madrid?

2 How old is the awesome Spain hero – 25, 26 or 27 years old?

3 True or False? Silva won the Premier League title in his first season at Man. City!

4 How many goals did Silva score at Euro 2012 – two, three or four?

5 True or False? Silva's header opened the scoring in the Euro 2012 Final against Italy!

2 POINTS FOR EACH CORRECT ANSWER

MY SCORE **10**

MYSTERY FACTPACK!

Fill in the gaps in these cool Xavi facts!

Height: **5ft 7ins**
Club:
Country: **Spain**
Age: **32**
Position: **Midfielder**
Value: **£20 million**
Boots:

5 POINTS FOR EACH CORRECT ANSWER

MY SCORE **10**

WORDSEARCH!

Find 20 Brazil and Argentina stars in this massive puzzle!

```
W X S D Y T B N G P L A V E Z Z I M D G Q M K M C P I
O R S I W Z R U W H X H Q G X J Z E S A R C J G J O J
H H S L I K P H G J B V H K M D Y S A G U E R O N L Y
D K S U W B R W G E I V P A T O B K W O H U B Q S X I
B H L R S C L B I Z D N M Z X G O O V W Z B V J N G Q
U S Z B Z Y I R S D F Z F O P R A M I R E S U E R G K
I Q G N K L U C I O S Q P Q K I D R V N A G N P V O V
D Z Q O E E U K I S X H H D M B I Z X L Z V T D G R O
U E T P P W W S H Q O D U A G U H T P Z Y A N X A N N
O A G S L S C R G Y O D L H M A R C E L O Z M A D X
T C S C H E L V A L S C S O K K V B N Q Q X Y R V L S
U H P I M H I G U A I N R O D B J G F B M E E D X H D
V K O J U J G V S H M E C Y K G F A N C N H A O P P R
X G N E H M E D W J M O G G Y L E N M X C Z N R Q K Z
K U V S Q R Y W G O N Y U S V M R S D S W N P A N A J
M Z V M O F H G R R O B I N H O T O A M A I C O N K H
D U Y V Z A B A L E T A K H W I A M Z Y I R E P V A S
```

Aguero	Higuain	Lucio	Mascherano	Ramires	**2 POINTS FOR EACH CORRECT ANSWER**
Damiao	Hulk	Luiz	Messi	Robinho	**MY SCORE**
Gago	Kaka	Maicon	Neymar	Romero	40
Ganso	Lavezzi	Marcelo	Pato	Zabaleta	

FLASHBACK!

5 POINTS FOR EACH CORRECT ANSWER

MY SCORE 20

Which Liverpool stars will want to forget these dodgy old pics?

THE LIVERPOOL STAR IS...

THE LIVERPOOL STAR IS...

THE LIVERPOOL STAR IS...

THE LIVERPOOL STAR IS...

ANSWERS ON PAGE 92

CROSSWORD!

2 POINTS FOR EACH CORRECT ANSWER

MY SCORE

50

ACROSS

2. Everton striker Nikica Jelavic plays for this international team! (7)

6. ____ Dzagoev, Russia star from Euro 2012! (4)

8. Republic Of Ireland manager at Euro 2012, Giovanni _____! (10)

10. Rock-solid Newcastle and Argentina centre-back, Fabricio _____! (9)

11. Tottenham defender signed from Ajax last summer! (10)

13. _____ Aguero, deadly Man. City and Argentina hitman! (6)

14. The Italian city where Fiorentina are based! (8)

15. Scorer of England's first goal at Euro 2012! (7)

16. The PFA Young Player Of The Year in 2012, ____ Walker! (4)

18. Last season's wicked Serie A champions! (8)

20. The sports giants that make T90 Laser IV and Tiempo Legend boots! (4)

23. Prem new boys from the south coast! (11)

24. Team that beat Cheltenham 2-0 in the League 2 Play-Off final last May! (5)

25. Premier League team nicknamed The Royals! (7)

DOWN

1. South coast team known as The Seagulls! (8)

3. Karim Benzema's international team! (6)

4. Barcelona's incredible home stadium! (3,4)

5. Makers of Liverpool's awesome 2012-13 kits! (7)

7. Top goalscorer in the Champions League last season! (6,5)

9. Ex-Chelsea megastar, _____ Drogba! (6)

12. Manchester, Norwich, Hull and Swansea! (4)

17. The main colour on Arsenal's super-cool away kit this season! (6)

19. West Ham _____! (6)

21. _____ Marin, Chelsea's summer signing from Werder Bremen! (5)

22. Euro 2012's Golden Boot winner! (6)

BALE

FACTPACK!

Club: Tottenham

Position: Winger

Age: 23

Height: 6ft 1in

Value: £40 million

Country: Wales

Did you know? Bale was the only Premier League star to be named in UEFA's Team Of The Year in 2011! What a legend!

STRANGE but true!

GOING UNDERGROUND!

Some of Britain's famous stadiums sit on really odd sites! Villa Park was built over a funfair, a police horse manure heap was cleared for Aberdeen's Pittodrie stadium and Exeter's St. James' Park was once a pig farm!

MATCH checks out the weirdest footy facts ever!

VAN'S THE MAN!

With Robin van Persie and Rafael van der Vaart, Holland always seem to play with a 'Van' in their squad! The last time they played without one was in a 2-0 win against China way back in 1996!

UNITED'S WORLD RECORD!

MEATY MOVE!

When Regal Horia bought defender Marius Cioara from UT Arad in 2006, they paid with 5kg of pork sausages! Cioara was so insulted that he quit footy and moved to Spain!

Between 1990 and 2004, seven video games were named after Prem giants Man. United! It's a Guinness World Record for a footy club!

MATCH!

GHOUL KEEPER!

Watford shot-stopper Manuel Almunia once thought his house was haunted! Built on the site of an old hospital, the keeper could hear chains being dragged around and his wife saw the ghost of a monk! Scary!

CRAZY CLUBS!

There are some hilarious club names around the world! Fotballaget Fart play their home games at the Fartbana in Norway, Wormatia Worms come from Germany and Argentina have a Club Deportivo Moron!

VFR WORMATIA 08 WORMS

FOTBALLAGET FART FFL 1934

HAT FACT!

You've seen Chelsea's Petr Cech wearing protective headgear – now check this guy out! Former Faroe Islands keeper Jens Knudsen used to wear a bobble hat after getting injured when he was younger!

SWEET SUCCESS!

Sir Alex Ferguson loves chewing gum, but rival Premier League manager Roberto Mancini enjoys munching on a different type of sweet! The class Man. City gaffer loves to chomp on Fruit Pastilles during matches! Legend!

STRANGE but true!

ENGLAND

Five South American countries have never played England in a full international! The Three Lions are still waiting to give Venezuela, Bolivia, Guyana, French Guiana and Suriname a game!

SICK!

NUTTER!

KIT CONFUSION!

MAD NAMES!

Check out these funny player names from down the years – Danny Diver, John Nutter, Johnny Moustache, Waldo Ponce, Gernot Sick and Dieter Stinka! England have even been captained by Harry Daft!

FERNANDO'S GROUND!

Ever wondered why Italy play in blue when their flag is red, white and green? We until the end of the Second World War, the Royal House of Savoy, whose official colour was blue, ruled Italy!

Spanish third division side Fuenlabrada play in the Fernando Torres Stadium! The class Chelsea and Spain striker was born in the area of Madrid in 1984!

WORLD CUP FINAL FASHION!

Belgian ref John Langenus, who was in charge of the first World Cup final between Uruguay and Argentina, wore a suit and tie for the match in 1930!

The Worst Kit Of 2012-13 award must surely go to Spain's Recreativo Huelva! Makers Hummel made a red shirt with white spots that some fans reckon makes the players look like Minnie Mouse!

SHIRT SHOCKER!

MOOSE ON THE LOOSE!

Back in the 1970s, Norway defender Svein Grondalen was ruled out of an international because he ran into a moose while out on a morning jog!

SNOW JOKE!

Way back in 1963, heavy snow and freezing conditions caused a Scottish Cup match between Airdrie and Stranraer to be postponed 33 times! Mental!

STRANRAER F.C. 1870

A.F.C. AIRDRIEONIANS

STAR OF 2012

MESSI

FACTPACK!

Club: Barcelona
Position: Striker
Age: 25
Height: 5ft 7ins
Value: £120 million
Country: Argentina
Did you know? Messi hit an incredible eight hat-tricks for Barcelona in 2011-12! That's a La Liga record!

Bayern Munich **1**

Muller 83

Chelsea **1**

Drogba 88   *Chelsea won 4-3 on penalties*

Date: May 19 **Venue:** Allianz Arena

Tournament: Champions League

What happened? Four years after heartbreak against Man. United, Chelsea finally won their first Champions League title! Thomas Muller put Bayern ahead, but Didier Drogba's bullet header sent the game into extra-time! Petr Cech saved Ivica Olic's penalty in the shoot-out, and Bastian Schweinsteiger hit the post, before Drogba fired Chelsea into the history books!

What Do You Remember?

1 True or False? Bayern Munich played the Champo League final in their home stadium!

2 Whose penalty did Chelsea keeper Petr Cech save in extra-time – Franck Ribery, Mario Gomez, Arjen Robben or Bastian Schweinsteiger?

3 True or False? The Champions League final was Didier Drogba's last match for Chelsea!

4 Name the Chelsea wonderkid who made his Champions League debut in the final!

5 Branislav Ivanovic, Raul Meireles, Ramires and which other Chelsea player was suspended for the final against Bayern?

SNAPPED!
EURO 2012 SPECIAL!

Fernando Torres **finally finds a way to get picked ahead of** Cesc Fabregas **– by booting him!**

I DIDN'T TOUCH YOU, CESC!

GET ME FREE!

HELP ME!

Poland**'s punishment for crashing out in the group stages looked well harsh!**

THAT REALLY HURT, NANDO!

PRESS UPS? NAH!

Nobody tells Mario Balotelli **what to do in training!**

Roy Hodgson **loves letting rip in training!**

AAHH... THAT'S BETTER!

GET MY FACE IN THE PIC!

Ronaldo **gets really mad when he sees a TV camera not pointing at him!**

THE BIG QUIZ!

flipped!

Which Premier League star has had his face messed up in this weird pic?

5 POINTS FOR THE CORRECT ANSWER

MY SCORE 5

5 QUESTIONS ON...

ANDRES INIESTA

1 How old is the amazing Barcelona star - 28, 29 or 30 years old?

2 True or False? The tricky Spain magician has played for Barça, Sevilla and Atletico Madrid!

3 Iniesta won the Champions League in 2006, 2009 and 2011, but which two English teams did Barcelona beat in those finals?

4 Which Holland keeper did Iniesta score past in the 2010 World Cup Final - Stekelenburg or Van der Sar?

5 True or False? The playmaker was named Player Of The Tournament at Euro 2012!

2 POINTS FOR EACH CORRECT ANSWER

MY SCORE 10

GOAL MACHINES!

Name these teams' Euro 2012 top goalscorer!

3 POINTS FOR EACH CORRECT ANSWER

MY SCORE 15

GERMANY

....

PORTUGAL

....

ITALY

....

SWEDEN

....

CROATIA

....

STAR JUMBLE!

Which players' names are scrambled up?

2 POINTS FOR EACH CORRECT ANSWER

MY SCORE 10

Deaf Snorer Torn

Drain Fried On

A Borrowed Twinkles

Needy Jewels Sir

Pentagon Senses She

BRAINBUSTERS!

How many questions can you answer?

1 Which three clubs were relegated from the Premier League in 2012?

2 Liverpool signed striker Fabio Borini from which club in July?

3 Who replaced Roy Hodgson as West Brom manager earlier this year?

4 Which Man. City hero assisted the most goals in the Prem last season?

5 Which team knocked Real Madrid out of last season's Champo League?

6 Who was sacked as Aston Villa manager back in May this year?

7 Name the ex-England and Stoke defender who returned to his hometown club last summer!

8 Which Prem club did Spurs' Gylfi Sigurdsson play for last season?

9 Steven Naismith plays for which country?

10 Shinji Kagawa joined Man. United from which German club?

4 POINTS FOR EACH CORRECT ANSWER

MY SCORE 40

FLASHBACK!

5 POINTS FOR EACH CORRECT ANSWER

MY SCORE 20

Which top Premier League strikers will want to forget these ancient pics?

THE PREM STRIKER IS...

THE PREM STRIKER IS...

THE PREM STRIKER IS...

THE PREM STRIKER IS...

ANSWERS ON PAGE 92

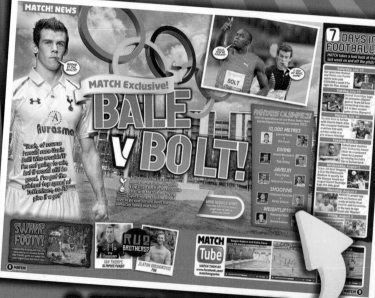

100% FOOTY ACTION EVERY WEEK!

MAD FOOTY FACTS!

COOL FOOTY GEAR!

MEGA-TOUGH QUIZZES!

PLAYER POSTERS!

CRAZY CARTOONS!

WIN PRIZES!

FUNNY PICS!

MATCH! 91

QUIZ ANSWERS!

Check out how well you did in MATCH's awesome football quizzes!

BIG QUIZ 1
PAGES 10-11

HEAD OF TWO HALVES:
David Luiz & Gareth Bale.
CLUB SHARERS: Man. City.
ROONEY QUIZ: 1. Everton; 2. True;
3. 27; 4. Ukraine; 5. 2010.
STAR JUMBLE: Eden Hazard; John Heitinga;
Brede Hangeland; Per Mertesacker; Carlos Cuellar.
WORDFIT:

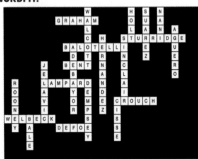

FLASHBACK: Sergio Ramos; Karim Benzema;
Mesut Ozil; Gonzalo Higuain.

SPOT THE DIFFERENCE
PAGE 12

1. 'The FA Cup' is missing on logo on banner;
2. 2012 now says 2011 on banner;
3. Michael Essien's wig is now green;
4. Gary Cahill's head is missing;
5. Roberto di Matteo's hand is missing;
6. Fernando Torres' badge is missing;
7. Didier Drogba's finger is missing;
8. Branislav Ivanovic's Samsung logo is missing;
9. Florent Malouda's boots are now blue;
10. 'Budweiser' is missing on advertising hoarding.

WORDSEARCH
PAGE 18

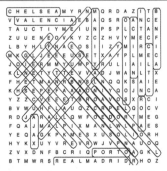

BIG QUIZ 2
PAGES 22-23

JOB SWAP: Steven Gerrard.
NAME THE MANAGER: Tottenham - Andre Villas-Boas;
Aston Villa - Paul Lambert; Norwich - Chris Hughton;
Liverpool - Brendan Rodgers; Barcelona - Tito Vilanova.
KOMPANY QUIZ: 1. Hamburg; 2. 26; 3. Belgium;
4. Premier League & FA Cup; 5. Thomas Vermaelen.
WHO AM I?: Papiss Cisse.
FLASHBACK: Ashley Cole; Joe Hart;
Jordan Henderson; John Terry.
WORDSEARCH:

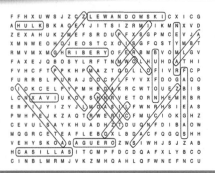

BIG QUIZ 3
PAGES 38-39

FLASHBACK: Paul Lambert.
MISSING PLAYERS:
AM - Xavi; FW - Cesc Fabregas.
TORRES QUIZ: 1. 28; 2. False - he started at
Atletico Madrid; 3. Liverpool; 4. QPR; 5. Three.
STAR JUMBLE: Clint Hill; Richard Dunne;
Scott Sinclair; Carlton Cole; Charlie Adam.
WORDFIT:

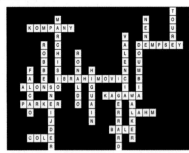

CAMERA SHY: Grant Holt; Micah Richards;
Joe Hart; Darren Bent.

WORDFIT
PAGE 42

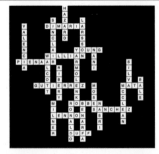

BIG QUIZ 4
PAGES 64-65

HEAD OF TWO HALVES:
Scott Parker & Ryan Giggs.
BOGUS BADGES: 1. Juventus; 2. West Ham;
3. Southampton; 4. Cardiff; 5. Real Madrid.
BALE QUIZ: 1. Cardiff; 2. 23;
3. Southampton; 4. False; 5. F50 adiZero.
WHO AM I?: Laurent Koscielny.
EURO GIANTS: Basel - Switzerland;
Nordsjaelland - Denmark; Malaga - Spain;
Braga -Portugal; Anzhi - Russia.
WORDFIT:

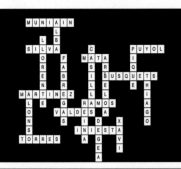

BIG QUIZ 5
PAGES 74-75

JOB SWAP: Gary Cahill.
SAGNA'S MAKEOVER: Demba Ba.
SILVA QUIZ: 1. Valencia; 2. 26; 3. False; 4. Two; 5. True.
MYSTERY FACTPACK: Barcelona & Adidas Predator LZ.
WORDSEARCH:

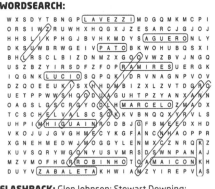

FLASHBACK: Glen Johnson; Stewart Downing;
Lucas; Charlie Adam.

CROSSWORD
PAGE 76

ACROSS: 2. Croatia; 6. Alan; 8. Trapattoni; 10. Coloccini;
11. Vertonghen; 13. Sergio; 14. Florence; 15. Lescott;
16. Kyle; 18. Juventus; 20. Nike; 23. Southampton;
24. Crewe; 25. Reading. **DOWN:** 1. Brighton; 3. France;
4. Nou Camp; 5. Warrior; 7. Lionel Messi; 9. Didier;
12. City; 17. Purple; 19. United; 21. Marko; 22. Torres.

BIG QUIZ 6
PAGES 88-89

FLIPPED: Phil Jones.
GOAL MACHINES: Germany - Mario Gomez; Portugal
- Cristiano Ronaldo; Italy - Mario Balotelli; Sweden
- Zlatan Ibrahimovic; Croatia - Mario Mandzukic.
INIESTA QUIZ: 1. 28; 2. False; 3. Arsenal &
Man. United; 4. Maarten Stekelenburg; 5. True.
STAR JUMBLE:
Fernando Torres; Rio Ferdinand; Robert Lewandowski;
Wesley Sneijder; Stephane Sessegnon.
BRAINBUSTERS: 1. Blackburn, Bolton & Wolves;
2. Roma; 3. Steve Clarke; 4. David Silva; 5. Bayern
Munich; 6. Alex McLeish; 7. Jonathan Woodgate;
8. Swansea; 9. Scotland; 10. Borussia Dortmund.
FLASHBACK: Luis Suarez; Danny Graham;
Djibril Cisse; Ricardo Vaz Te.

MY SCORE

/800

CISSE

FACTPACK!

Club: Newcastle

Position: Striker

Age: 27

Height: 6ft

Value: £18 million

Country: Senegal

Did you know? The lethal striker scored 13 goals in his first 13 Premier League games for The Magpies!

did you know?

Loads of cool facts and stats to impress your mates!

19 Loads of big-time Prem stars hit hat-tricks in 2011-12! There were 19 in total – Demba Ba, Wayne Rooney and Robin van Persie managed to bag two trebles each!

54 They might be down in the Third Division in Scotland this season, but Rangers have won the most league titles in the world! They've lifted an incredible 54 trophies!

3 Liverpool striker Fabio Borini has played for Brendan Rodgers three times! The Reds boss was his coach at Chelsea reserves and Swansea, before signing him for the Anfield side!

Martin Jol must have told his Fulham team to keep it clean last season! They were the only Prem side not to be shown a red card!

99,252 Nearly 100,000 fans went home disappointed from the Nou Camp last season as Barcelona lost 2-1, and the title, to Real Madrid!

7 West Ham star Ravel Morrison complained of toothache while on a pre-season tour of Germany. He flew home as he needed to have SEVEN teeth taken out! Ouch!

Olivier Giroud and Laurent Koscielny were team-mates at French side Tours a few years before joining Arsenal!

Shinji Kagawa became the first Japanese player to join Man. United when he arrived at Old Trafford from Borussia Dortmund back in June 2012!